Operation Night Monster

Written by
Paul Shipton

Illustrated by
Ben Mounsey

Ali was playing with his new Rocky Robot toy. Rocky was battling the monsters of Planet Zyborg. One of the monsters was Ali's old teddy bear, Fred. Fred wasn't much good at this game – he didn't look at all monstrous.

Ali's big brother, Jamal, stuck his head round the door. "Don't play monster games too close to bedtime!" he said.

"Why not?" asked Ali.

"Because then you'll dream about REAL monsters!" said Jamal. "And we all know you're scared of monsters!"

"I'm NOT scared of monsters!" Ali said.

Even so, at bedtime, Ali did a 'Monster Check'.
He looked under the bed. He looked in the bed.
He held his nose and looked through all his
dirty clothes. But he didn't find any monsters
there ...

Ali climbed into bed. Fred came too.
He always did. Sometimes, Ali thought that
Fred could talk to him.

"I am a *bit* scared of monsters," Ali whispered.

"Hmmm," said Fred. "You won't be afraid
if you think about something funny. Just
think about … hippos playing football!
They wouldn't be much good at throw-ins!"

8

Ali tried, but he kept on thinking about you-know-whats … monsters.

Then he heard a voice in the dark.
"Pssst! Hey, kid!"
"Who's there?" said Ali.
"It's me, Rocky Robot! Don't listen to that soft toy!" he said. "If I spot a monster, I'll catch it! I'll bash it! I'll clobber it and smash it!"

"What do you think, Fred?" Ali asked.
The old bear thought it over. "Hmmm … we'll see."

Ali fell asleep.

It wasn't long before Ali woke up.

Something was wrong ...

The wardrobe door was open, just a bit.

What if a you-know-what was in there?

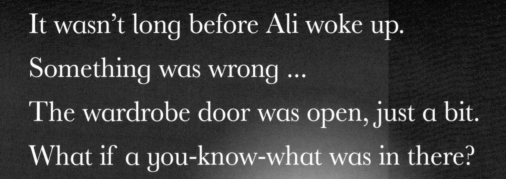

"Don't worry," said Fred. "Think about something funny, like dolphins playing computer games!

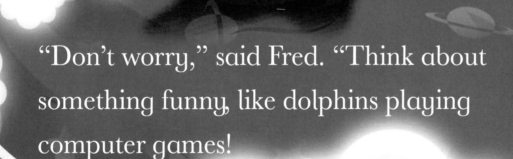

Ali jumped out of bed, slammed the wardrobe door shut, and jumped back into bed before anything could get him.

But Ali couldn't get back to sleep.

"I need the loo," he thought. "I really need the loo, but it's all the way along the landing!"

"Don't worry," said Fred. "Just think about …"

"I can't think about anything except monsters!" cried Ali.

"Hmmm," said Fred. "OK, then think about *silly* monsters on skateboards!"

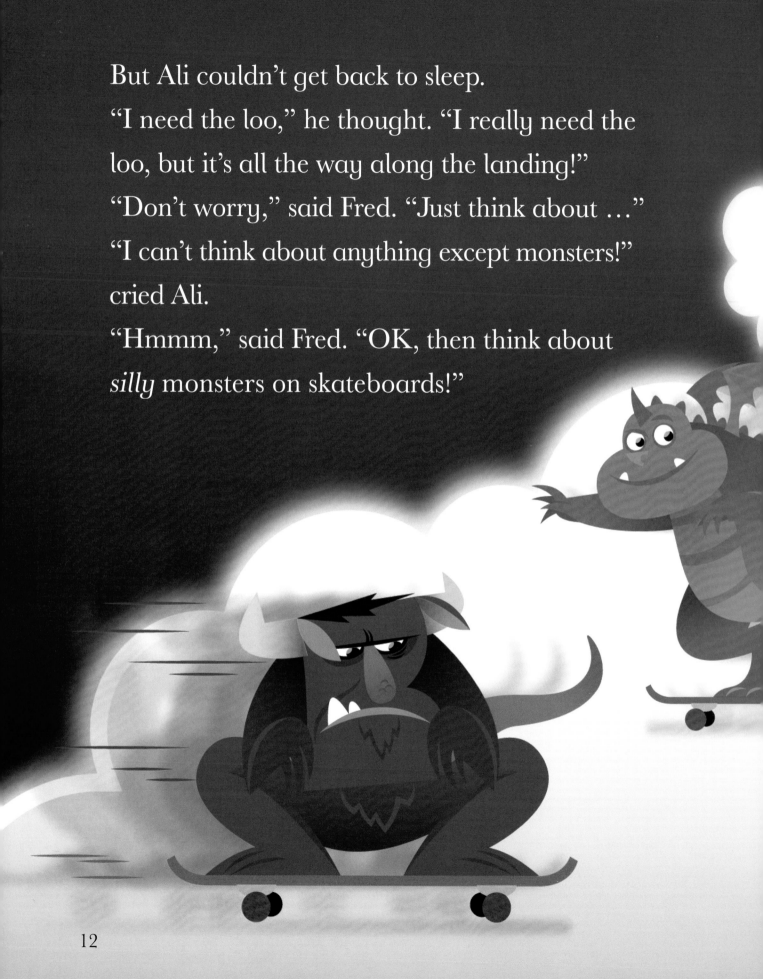

14

Ali tiptoed out of his bedroom, with both toys under one arm and the rolled-up comic in his other hand.

He took one step forward, then another and another. But when he reached the end of the landing, he saw … something.

Something big.
Something dark.
Something … monstrous!

18

STAMP!

OW!

Ali saw a flash
of spotty pants.

The monster started whizzing back along the landing … on Ali's skateboard!

The monster zoomed into Jamal's room, and crashed into the bed.
"OW!" it yelled again.

Ali thought he recognised the heap under Jamal's dressing gown …

"Ali? I thought you were a ..." Jamal moaned, rubbing his head.

"Ha!" said Ali. "You thought I was a monster!"

"I didn't!" said Jamal.

"Did! Did! Did!" laughed Ali.

22

Then Mum called out,

What's going on?

"Nothing," Jamal answered quickly. "Ali thought he saw a burglar, but it was just me going to the loo."

Ali got back into bed.

"That was a fantastic success!" said Rocky.

"Good thing you had me there for Operation Night Monster!"

Ali remembered his brother zooming along the landing on a skateboard. He smiled.

"What do you think, Fred?" he asked.

But Fred was already asleep.

And soon, so was Ali.

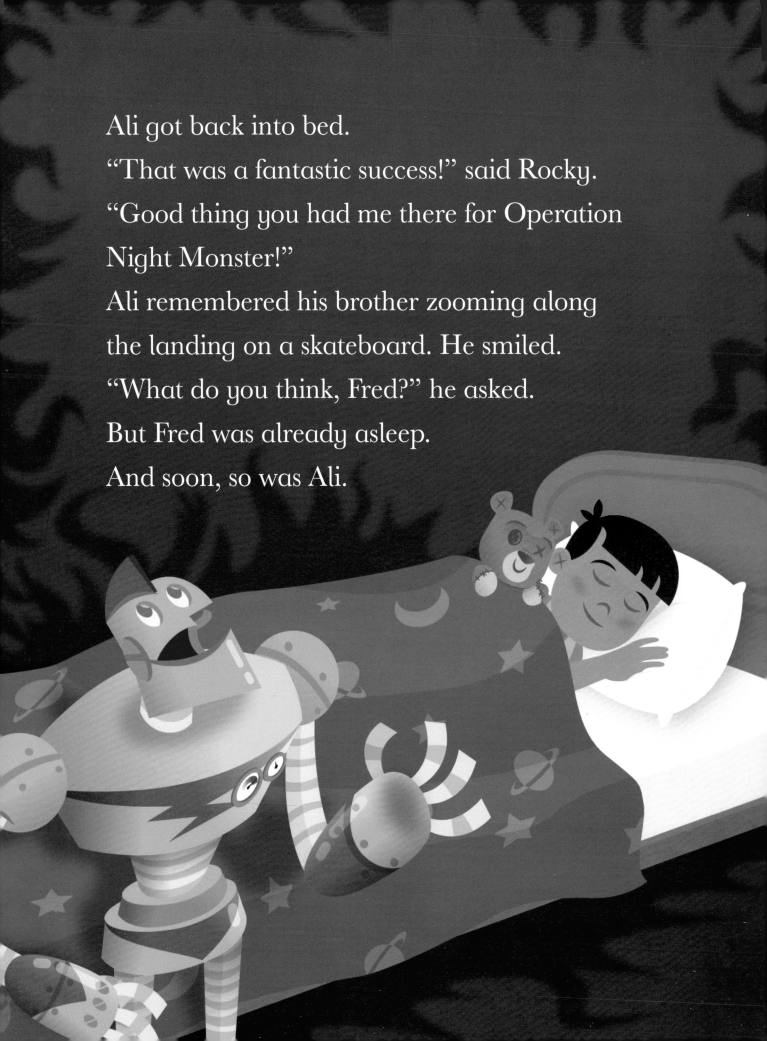